Poodles & Doodles

Poems About Dogs

Leslie C. Halpern

Cautious Optimist Publishing
Oviedo, Florida

Poodles & Doodles: Poems About Dogs
by Leslie C. Halpern

ISBN: 978-0-9993763-4-8 (paperback)
ISBN: 978-0-9993763-5-5 (Kindle)
ISBN: 978-0-9993763-6-2 (case laminate)

For bulk sales, contact:
Cautious Optimist Publishing
CautiousOptimistPub@gmail.com
Oviedo Florida

Cover & Interior design and production by Rik Feeney / usabookcoach@gmail.com

Permissions:
Cover Photo 127162776 © Windowsontheworldphotography | Dreamstime.com

Dedication

To Snickerdoodle, Brina, Ditza,
Bagel and Arnold.

Poodles & Doodles

Acknowledgments

My sincere appreciation goes to Rik Feeney of Richardson Publishing for his expert assistance in design and production.

Thank you to the talented members of Orlando Area Poets (a chapter of Florida State Poets Association) who critiqued many of these pieces and helped me clip, shave, and pluck excess verbiage from the poems to give them an expertly groomed appearance.

A few of these poems were previously published in other books.

Silly Sleepytime Poems (Cautious Optimist Publishing, 2017): "Animals Dream, Too."

Frogs, Hogs, Puppy Dogs (Cricket Cottage Publishing, 2013): "Almost Everything," "Fleas," "The Sunny Spot," "Squeaker of the House," and "Fussy Eater."

Contents

Poodles & Doodles

Introduction

I thought I knew a lot about how to raise, train, and befriend a dog until I adopted my newest puppy. Not quite the level of a dog whisperer, I believed myself to have at least achieved a low-volume dog mumbler status when relating to my beloved furry friends. I'd cherished the poodles I had raised from puppyhood to adulthood, and had provided them with a stable, loving environment. I'd even been a successful step-owner-in-law (once removed) for someone else's aging dog.

So, I was unprepared for the challenge of Snickerdoodle. A literal hot mess of a dog is something you might step in accidentally while mowing the grass, but in this case I'm speaking figuratively. My miniature schnoodle puppy, Snickerdoodle, is undeniably a hot mess of a dog. In fact, I'm considering changing her name to Snickerdon't. It seems like the words "no," "down," and "don't" (usually shouted on the brink

11

of an elimination disaster, shredding of an unpaid invoice, or consumption of a squirming blood worm) are my main means of communicating these days.

It didn't start out that way, of course. When I first saw the nameless big-eyed, ginger-colored ball of fluff from the breeder's selection of pups, I liked her immediately. While the other puppies slept, barked, fought, or sniffed fallen poop, this one poked her tiny snout through the bars and silently pleaded with me to take her home, give her love, and name her after a cookie.

When I asked to hold her, the nice man said, "She's a schnoodle—half schnauzer, half poodle—and will give you 15 years of cuddling, joy, and unconditional love." It took only 15-minutes of cuddling, joy, and unconditional love to convince me this calm little snuggler was the puppy for me.

Schnoodles are bred to combine the best qualities of both breeds, but occasionally it backfires and the opposite occurs. What the nice man didn't tell me was that apart from being physically adorable, schnoodles may get the worst of both breeds, with the high-strung sensibilities of a poodle (i.e., they pee when excited) and the strong will and loud bark factor of a schnauzer (i.e., they're possessive and territorial).

Once she settled into my home, Snickerdoodle growled for her supper, barked at strangers, damaged expensive items, and urinated indiscriminately (all very much like a man I once dated). The conniving pooch was no calm little snuggler like she pretended to be when we met. That was merely an act to get adopted. She revealed herself to be a feisty mischief maker with a tiny bladder and no impulse control who took great delight in nipping at my bare ankles and chomping her needle-like teeth into my silk blouses.

After reading several dog-training books without success, I joined an online schnoodle support group. In addition to having trouble spelling the breed name correctly, we all endured similar problems with our adorable dogs. But I'm the only one who had all the problems combined into one dog. Therefore, no definitive answers were provided by other owners. My next step was enrolling Snickerdoodle in a puppy obedience school. At the first class, I learned she was by far the naughtiest dog there. She shrieked her unhappiness to the other students and suffered a series of anxiety attacks. At the end of our first session, the instructor said: "Well, she's not the *worst* dog I've ever seen."

I thought they might kick us out of school and return my money, but instead they set up a special secluded corner with barricades where Snickerdoodle and I were sequestered for the remainder of the six-week course. By the final class when the students were tested and awarded graduation certificates, the instructor was barely even speaking to us—much less praising Snickerdoodle's potential to be a normal dog.

I brought my son with me to graduation night, thinking his presence might give Snickerdoodle more confidence. She obviously loves him because whenever he comes over to the house for a visit, she jumps on him excitedly and empties her bladder near his size 13 feet. Unfortunately, even with him in attendance, my hot mess of a dog did what hot things do. She suffered a meltdown.

During the testing portion, Snickerdoodle barked at other dogs as they quietly waited for instructions. She growled at the school's director who made his first appearance on that final night. She energetically jumped on the instructor when she was supposed to stay down and touch the offered hand. After passing a few of the initial exams, she failed one test after another as the class progressed and her behavior regressed. It's like she forgot every new response she'd learned over the past six weeks.

Just before the presentation of certificates and official graduation ceremony, poor Snickerdoodle couldn't take the pressure any longer and launched the final phase of her meltdown. She peed, pooped, lost a tooth, and bit my son on the nose. Even so, my ill-mannered little girl was still awarded a bag of treats and a gold-seal certificate stating that she completed a class in "Small Paw Etiquette." Basically, she passed the course by showing up to classes and being a puppy. I'm guessing if they have an alumni reunion party, Snickerdoodle's name won't be on the guest list.

So, this is the challenge I face with the newest addition to my family: give her up to an animal shelter; keep her and have a nervous breakdown; hire a dog trainer to come to the house and work with her individually; or write about the experience to put it into perspective. Throughout my life, I've attempted to find the deeper meaning in challenges—to identify the emotional truth hidden beneath distracting superficial details. And when that fails, I look for the humor. Sometimes if I'm lucky, I discover truth and humor. That's my goal with *Poodles & Doodles: Poems About Dogs*—to remember the variety of experiences (positive and negative) associated with having a dog of any breed and to reveal the curious and comical parallels between us and our canine companions for readers of all ages.

Leslie C. Halpern, March 31, 2019

Play Time

Thieving Schnoodle

She loves to nip and bite,
and grab things with her teeth.
Then she's soon out of sight.
Find which bed she's beneath.

Chewing shoes, socks, slippers,
soggy towels from the beach,
scissors, nose hair clippers,
whatever she can reach.

Everything has teeth marks
from compulsive chewing.
She chomps instead of barks,
like most dogs are doing.

Sheets and pillowcases,
paper napkins, tissues—
around the house she races.
Clearly she has issues.

Frenetic Random Activity

Zoomies
wild, unpredictable,
crouching, running, colliding
suffering from an extreme puppy moment
panting, slowing, calming
tired, exhausted,
Sleep

Play Time Haiku #1

rubber balls, rawhide,
squeaky toys with chewy nubs
she prefers my shoes

Play Time Haiku #2

eyes apologize
soft white tummy now exposed
my new dress in shreds

Play Time Haiku #3

one washcloth missing
two shoe inserts, three black socks
I lost or dog found

Leslie C. Halpern

Half-Price Puppy

adorable balls of fur
with huge anime eyes
black dot noses

four tiny paws
balancing unstable
little mops of hair

one pair of sad eyes
catches my attention
leads me to her

she embraces my neck
sinks claws into sweater
melts heart with warm belly

salesman offers discount
half off for that one
won't eat, won't play

nobody wants her
clearance priced poodle
been here for weeks

(continued next page)

now *my* adorable ball of fur
with huge anime eyes
black dot nose

eats treats, stays, plays
loves enough for two dogs
for half the price of one

There Once Was a Poodle Named Joy

There once was a poodle named Joy
who resented being a toy.
"I'm a dog, not a doll,
so just throw the darn ball.
And don't paint my nails, I'm a boy."

A Large Goldendoodle Named Higgins

A large goldendoodle named Higgins
had feet that were certainly big'uns.
He could swat away flies,
hold up 15 French fries,
and yield bugs and worms from his diggin's.

There Once Was a Whoodle Named Kate

There once was a whoodle named Kate
who walked with a lopsided gait.
Though a nice disposition,
feet in second position—
her ballet dancing wasn't great.

Meal Time

Reflection

My adopted toy poodle
has curly hair like mine.
People say we look the same,
and I think that's just fine.

Over the years, I've watched
her personality quirks.
Some might call them problems,
but for me they're more like perks.

She lines kibbles in neat rows
in multiples of four.
If one gets out of place,
you'll hear this poodle roar.

But she doesn't bark or growl
when something's wrong with her.
She doesn't even whimper
from a rectal thermometer.

(continued next page)

She pats her squeaky ball
five times before she plays.
Tell her to stay and she comes –
and then say come, she stays.

The sound of running water
always terrifies her.
Dried worms are her onion rings,
a yummy appetizer.

She wakes me up at 3:00 a.m.,
and thinks it's time to eat.
She's ready for a full-course meal,
not just a doggy treat.

This girly girl hates wet paws
and hops across each puddle,
yet rolls in mud and poop,
and then comes close to cuddle.

(continued next page)

Leslie C. Halpern

Thunderstorms make her shiver,
must bring some trauma back.
Her trips to see the groomer
prompt an anxiety attack.

Now that she's a senior dog,
her paws and ears are smelly.
Her skinny legs must balance
a large protruding belly.

She doesn't jump or dance as much.
Her "puppy moments" are long gone,
but she's still as odd as ever
and in some ways twice the fun.

She's the most neurotic dog –
behavioral disaster,
not like other people's pets:
a rare breed like her master.

Kibble Nibbler

Unsatisfied
parched, empty
growing, niggling, gnawing
bowl filled to the brim with kibbles
salivating, eating, enjoying
full, snuggly
Satisfied

Pica Puppy

My little dog has pica,
but still has a joyful time.
He eats only puppy food –
no more dirt, hair, dust, or grime.

He doesn't like the muzzle
but must soon get used to it.
Strapped across his schnoodle nose,
he will always pitch a fit.

It's tough to have such a dog
who eats anything he sees.
And he has other problems,
such as bad breath, warts, and fleas.

Fussy Eater

My puppy will eat stickers,
postage stamps, letters, labels,
cardboard boxes, paper bags,
and things on kitchen tables.

Everything goes in her mouth.
She will swallow it down whole.
The only food she doesn't like
is whatever's in her bowl.

Meal Time Haiku #1

human grade chicken
designer bowls and placemat
puppy chomps on rocks

Meal Time Haiku #2

pill hidden inside
pungent cheese masks scent and taste
yet he still finds it

Meal Time Haiku #3

gratitude expressed
there's no need for words of thanks
after-meal snuggle

Perspective

A furry disheveled little mess
of brown, white, black, and gold,
she sat in a cage with a sign
announcing breed and price.
She wouldn't play or eat –
just held on through the day
anxiously awaiting adoption.

I guided her through puppyhood,
soiled carpets, chewed table legs.
She comforted me after surgery,
through a divorce, my empty nest.
Now I feed her six meals a day
on a special restrictive diet,
spend hundreds on her meds.

She licks my hand after eating,
leans against me while I read.
I know softness of her belly,
feel of her scratchy paws,
waxy innards of her ears.
I soothe her during storms,
hold her until shuddering subsides.

(continued next page)

She's my welcome home beacon;
an eleven-pound perpetual puppy
despite greying hair and early arthritis—
a drooling expression of unconditional love.
On our walks, hawks screech excitedly
upon seeing her from light pole perches,
considering my best friend a lunch option.

Introduction to a Strawberry

It's not a bug; it doesn't crawl.
It doesn't roll; it's not a ball.
It fell from a cup
near this confused pup,
and the smell is so wonderful.

Nap Time

Mystery of the Squeaky Yawn

She stretches her mouth open to full capacity, not to
Question my authority, but to emit a high-pitched yawn.
Unlike humans, who may offer a soft accompanying sigh,
Each doggy yawn sounds like it needs lubricating oil.
Already the center of attention, she may whine for more.
Kids who whine aren't cute, yet we love a dog's squeak.

Stillness of Night

Asleep
calm, quiet
relaxing, renewing, dreaming
unmistakable sound of retching near my ear
panicking, screaming, running
stressed, noisy
Awake

Fleas

My little puppy has some fleas
on his belly, ears, and knees

above his whiskers, near his eyes
on his tail, around his thighs,

on his paws, his back, his head
and since last night, they're in my bed.

The Sunny Spot

I like the way my little dog
sleeps in the sunny spot.
When home is dark and wintry cold,
she'll find the place that's hot.

A tiny sliver of sunshine
is all that needs to please
my furry little friend as she
recharges batteries.

Nap Time Haiku #1

she snores on my lap
I write poems about her
she must find them dull

Nap Time Haiku #2

tiny toy poodle
my seven-pound curly girl
snores like an old man

Nap Time Haiku #3

dream ends abruptly
a tongue licks my eyes and face
neighbor's lawn awaits

Let Sleeping Dogs Lie

My right hand cramped.
My arm is numb.
I have a splinter
in my thumb.

My big toe itches.
My throat is dry.
I'd like to sit,
but here I lie.

My eyes are tearing.
My nose is hissing.
There's a show on TV
that I'm missing.

If you think I mind,
you'd be mistaken.
Dog's asleep on me—
must not awaken.

Animals Dream, Too

When my puppy sleeps
her paws start twitching
like she has a bite
that's started itching.

Or maybe she's dreaming
of chasing a kitten
and not a mosquito
that's recently bitten.

Between sleepy growls,
and moves, it would seem
that without a doubt
my puppy can dream.

Leslie C. Halpern

There Once Was a Schnoodle Named Ginny

There once was a schnoodle named Ginny
whose torso was quite long and skinny.
She jumped onto laps
expecting her naps.
She thought she was toy, not a mini.

51

A Labradoodle Named Breezy

A labradoodle named Breezy
became asthmatic and wheezy.
As his coat did not shed,
he could sleep in their bed,
until *he* became too sneezy.

Bath Time

Doggy Diagnosis

I think my dog has ADD
although she can remember me,
she can't recall an old command
like *sit*, *stay*, *down*, or *touch my hand*.

She looks at me with huge black eyes
but does not seem to realize
that bath time is required each week
to clean up every poop and leak.

She jumps up like the floor's on fire
each day reaching that much higher.
She cannot seem to concentrate.
Perhaps I need to medicate.

Dogs and Water

Paddle
instinctive, comical
splashing, moving, swimming
inexplicably terrified of cleaning routine
straining, kicking, fighting
anxious, alarmed
Bath

Almost Everything

I love most things about my dog.
She's the greatest pet, I think.
I love her from her wagging tail
to her tiny tongue that's pink.

I love to watch her run and play,
scratch her itches, eat and drink.
I love her yippy little bark,
but don't like her doggone stink.

Bath Time Haiku #1

paws stink like Fritos
smelly belly, sardine breath
someone needs a bath

Bath Time Haiku #2

bath time dramedy
evil vacuum cleaner's child
scary blow dryer

Bath Time Haiku #3

groomer's report card:
ears are hairy and waxy
can *she* pass that test?

Squeaker of the House

I dress my dog in baby clothes,
clean her teeth and floss.
I rub a tissue on her nose
And brush her fur to gloss.

I cook her meals, make sure she's fed,
put ribbons in her hair
paint her nails fire engine red—
give tender loving care.

She has designer squeaky toys,
a padded stroller when we walk.
Her life is filled with countless joys.
I've started teaching her to talk.

An Old Aussiedoodle Named Sadie

An old Aussiedoodle named Sadie
lived life as a dignified lady
except when they wiped her,
for she wore a diaper,
and pooped in her pants like a baby.

Any Time

Snickerdoodle

Soft golden curls
adorn my schnoodle.
Bushy eyebrows,
still one-half poodle.

Her skinny legs
look just like noodles.
She snickers when
she leaves her doodles.

Doggy-Gate Scramble

Under
low inhibitions
stretching, scooting, sliding
the great doggy-gate escape artist
jumping, lunging, pouncing
high expectations
Over

Hermit Crabs

My neighbors live like hermits,
tucked away inside their beautiful
two-story exoskeleton sanctuary
with a perfectly manicured
lawn that makes mine look like
property that's been abandoned.
Home provides their workplace,
and play space, away from the rat race
in the workaday world around them.
Safe in their shell, they venture outside
only when my dog needs to poop.

Any Time Haiku #1

what just happened here
benign surprise from inside
puppy's first hiccups

Any Time Haiku #2

designer puppies
extra cost for mixed-breed dogs
used to be called mutts

Any Time Haiku #3

she growls at mirror
ferocious cockapoo
snarls back at her

A Standard Poodle
Maintained a Stance

A standard poodle maintained a stance
that her ancestors all started in France.
She denied they were German,
declared them as vermin.
"I have my standards," she said with a glance.

A Labradoodle Named Clyde

A labradoodle named Clyde
harbored much conflict inside.
"I was a retriever,
now through a crossbreeder,
an allergy-friendly guide."

Leslie C. Halpern

Law of Attraction

Chewed up table legs and chairs,
plush toys, balls, and teddy bears.

Shredded paper, carpet stains—
so much loss, so many gains.

Missing squeakers, messy crates,
boo boos, accidents, mistakes.

My puppy's tail wags with glee
matching what she gets from me.

All the money spent on vets
returns as love from our pets.

Author Biography

Based in Central Florida, Leslie C. Halpern is an award-winning poet, essayist, and entertainment journalist with more than 4,000 published articles, and author of several books of nonfiction and poetry. Her work has appeared in hundreds of print and online publications, including *The Hollywood Reporter*, *Daily Variety*, *Orlando Sentinel*, *Storytelling Magazine*, *The Journal of Graduate Liberal Studies*, *Encore Prize Poems 2018*, *Revelry*, *Haikuniverse*, *Scifaikuest*, *Poetry to Feed the Spirit*, and *Other Orlandos*.

She maintains a pop culture and entertainment blog called "Seen It, Done It, Reviewed It: The Blog" at www.lesliehalpern.com/blog, and serves as president of Orlando Area Poets, the local chapter of Florida State Poets Association. Leslie earned a Master of Liberal Studies degree from Rollins College and a B.A. in Journalism from the University of Kentucky. She has won dozens of awards for her writing, including First Place Humorous Poetry Award from the National Federation of State Poetry Societies, Editor's Award for Poetry from The Gwendolyn Brooks

Writers Association of Florida, Distinguished Service Award from Florida Literacy Coalition, and Outstanding Contribution to Literacy Award from Seminole State College.

Also by Leslie C. Halpern

POETRY

Silly Sleepytime Poems
(978-0999376300)

Frogs, Hogs, Puppy Dogs: Funny Children's Poems About Animal Friends
(978-0692258996)

Shakes, Cakes, Frosted Flakes: Funny Children's Poems About Table Manners
(978-0615883267)

Rub, Scrub, Clean the Tub: Funny Children's Poems About Self-Image
(978-1478254751)

NONFICTION

Scantily Clad Truths: Essays on Life with Clothes (and without)
(978-0-9993763-3-1)

200 Love Lessons from the Movies: Staying Moonstruck for Life
(978-1630761370)

Reel Romance: The Lovers' Guide to the 100 Best Date Movies
(978-1589790643)

Passionate About Their Work: 151 Celebrities, Artists, and Experts on Creativity
(978-1593935481)

Dreams on Film: The Cinematic Struggle Between Art and Science
(978-0786415960)

***

If you enjoyed this book or any of Leslie's other publications, please share the love and post a review at your favorite online book retailer or site for book lovers.

www.LeslieHalpern.com

Ordering Information

Cautious Optimist Publishing
Oviedo, Florida

CautiousOptimistPub@gmail.com

www.LeslieHalpern.com

www.ingramcontent.com/pod-product-compliance
Lightning Source LLC
Chambersburg PA
CBHW021218020426
42331CB00003B/362